BE ENCOURAGED

A Daily Devotional, Volume 1

Gregory A. Johnson

ISBN: 1468172956
ISBN 13: 9781468172959
Library of Congress Control Number: 2012902017
CreateSpace, North Charleston, South Carolina

Visit the author's website:
http://www.GregoryAJohnson.com

This book is dedicated to my parents,
Elmer and Lois Johnson,
for a lifetime of encouragement.

Table of Contents

ACKNOWLEGEMENTS

I am thankful for God's Word—the Bible. It gives us much needed guidance and encouragement for our journey as we read it daily and allow the Holy Spirit to apply it to our lives, our circumstances, and our situations.

I am thankful for prayer; it is truly a privilege that God has given to us so that we may talk directly with Him.

I am thankful for people who have devotion to God's Word and prayer.

INTRODUCTION

One of my favorite Scriptures in the Bible says, "And let us consider how to stir up one another to love and good works, not neglecting to meet together, as is the habit of some, but encouraging one another, and all the more as you see the Day drawing near" (Hebrews 10:24-25).

Some pastors have utilized this Scripture throughout the years, albeit with good intentions, to impress on their congregation the importance of church attendance. In over twenty-one years of pastoring, I have also utilized it within that context. Although church attendance is important for those physically able to go, I believe we have missed the full implication of this Scripture and have restricted "meet together" to coincide with the walls of a church building and the confines of a church service. Let us never forget that we can also "meet together" in a home, a school, or a workplace: any location can be used to come together for service. We can "meet together" on the Internet and on the phone. We can even "meet together" within the pages of this book.

I believe we receive the full meaning of this wonderful Scripture by not restricting ourselves to a certain meeting location. Instead, we should take advantage of **all** avenues of "meeting together" to fulfill the message of this Scripture: that we should encourage and stir one another to love and good works in all areas of life.

It is my intent to meet with you in the pages of this devotional book, stirring you to love and good works while encouraging you on your journey. I'm sure that you have noticed that this journey we are on, called life, is a marathon. Endurance for the journey requires inspiration and encouragement. My prayer is that each of you will be encouraged and find renewed strength for your journey within these pages.

Know that you are loved,

Gregory A. Johnson
http://www.GregoryAJohnson.com

BE A STAR FOR JESUS

Have you ever been in the country away from city lights on a clear summer night when the moon is less than half-full? The stars are so bright, twinkling, and glistening, and you can see so many more of them than you can in a well-lit city. It is one of those spectacular sights that reminds all of creation that God is the all-powerful Creator. I can sit under a sky like that for hours and praise God in all of His splendor and glory.

Our culture today is darkened by sin; it is crooked, twisted, and greedy. We can choose to grumble and complain about how bad things are, or we can be like the stars whose light pierces the darkness. The choice is ours, but we will not make a difference by only talking about how bad things have become.

We are to be like the stars that shine brightly, reflecting the Son. As we do, those around us will marvel in what God can do in a person who submits their life to Him in total abandonment. The creation will know that there is a Creator.

Beloved, be like a star on a clear night, reflecting the light of the Son in the midst of a dark world. Twinkle, twinkle little star...

SCRIPTURE:

"Do all things without grumbling or questioning, that you may be blameless and innocent, children of God without blemish in the midst of a crooked and twisted generation, among whom you shine as lights in the world" (Philippians 2:14-15).

PRAYER:

My awesome Creator, I pray today that you will help me shine in the midst of darkness. It is easy for me to grumble, complain, and question. Help me reflect the light of Jesus. As others see the light of Jesus through me, draw them to Him. I pray this in Jesus' name. Amen.

VICTORY!

There is one constant theme throughout the entire Bible—VICTORY! Because of His love and grace, God grants victory for His children. Life here on earth can be a battle as we try to live for the LORD, but we are afforded victory, and our victory is in Him.

Beloved, your victory today is found in Jesus. Follow Him with your whole being and victory is yours.

SCRIPTURE:

"No weapon that is fashioned against you shall succeed, and you shall confute every tongue that rises against you in judgment. This is the heritage of the servants of the LORD and their vindication from me, declares the LORD" (Isaiah 54:17).

PRAYER:

Father, I thank you for the victory you have given us through Jesus Christ. I pray for those today who are facing persecution in the home, workplace, schoolhouse, or wherever they are doing what is right and good as they follow Christ. I pray for those living in lands where their life is in danger because of their faith in Jesus. Encourage each one today, Father.

Strengthen us all by your Holy Spirit, giving each of us reaffirmation of the victory that has already been afforded us at the cross of Christ, including our ultimate victory which is to come. I pray in Jesus' name, Amen.

DAY 3

HOW TO LOOK AT YOUR CIRCUMSTANCES DIFFERENTLY

I may be tired, confused, and even somewhat depressed when I go into my place of prayer, but I'm strengthened, enlightened, and my heart is full of thanksgiving when I come out. I go in as one person and come out as another. I'm renewed in His presence.

If you pray, you know what I am talking about. You have experienced the same. Do you know why it happens?

Prayer changes us. Even if our circumstances are the same, after we spend time around the throne of God in prayer, we are changed. When we enter our place of prayer, we are not the same person as we are when we come out.

Prayer is powerful. When I pray, I know that God hears my cries. The very One who created everything by His spoken word listens to you and me. Why? Because He loves us, and He cares for us.

Pray on, Beloved. Pray on. It will change you, and you will look at your circumstances differently.

SCRIPTURE:

"Blessed be the LORD! For he has heard the voice of my pleas for mercy. The LORD is my strength and my shield; in him my heart trusts, and I am helped; my heart exults, and with my song I give thanks to him" (Psalms 28:6-7).

PRAYER:

Father, I thank you for the privilege of prayer that you give us. The time we spend with you is life changing. I know that you are looking out for my best interests, and I trust you. My heart is full of thanksgiving today because you give me a joy that is unspeakable and full of glory. Please continue to change me as I pray. Help me to look at my circumstances differently, fully trusting you to strengthen and protect me in the midst of everything. Instead of being burdened and anxious, help me be patient as I pray, allowing you to work in each situation. I pray in the name of Jesus. Amen.

TAKEN OUT OF THIS WORLD

For many years, it has been popular to trace a family's ancestry back as far as one can go. There are many resources available now, including the Internet, which makes information for genealogical research more readily available.

The genealogy of Noah is given in Genesis 5:1-32 of the Bible and traces all the way back to Adam. It is interesting to note that after stating the name of each ancestor and years of his life, it is always stated that the individual died, except in one instance—Enoch. It does not state that Enoch died, but instead it says "God took him."

Enoch was close to God, and God enjoyed his company very much. They would walk with each other every day. I imagine God waited for Enoch to awaken each day so they could spend time together. One day, God just took Enoch into His presence to be with Him for all eternity. Enoch bypassed death.

God has made a way for us to have eternal life through Jesus Christ. We can walk with Him every day, and one day He will take us to be with Him forever. God taking Enoch typifies the great gathering in the sky with the LORD that is to come for Christ followers.

Beloved, as you follow Christ, you walk with God. We can walk with Him every day. God loves your company so much that one day, as you follow Christ, He will take you to be with Him for all eternity. The best is yet to come!

SCRIPTURE:

"Enoch walked with God, and he was not, for God took him" (Genesis 5:24).

PRAYER:

Father, I thank you for eternal life with you that is afforded through Jesus Christ. The great gathering with Him in the sky, as declared in your Word, could happen today. We could experience today what Enoch experienced many years ago — to be taken away with you. Help me to stay focused on that which is to come while never losing sight of the One I follow—Jesus Christ. I've been distracted before, and I desire not to be distracted again. Help me keep my eyes fixed on Jesus today. I pray it in His name. Amen.

HOW TO LIVE WITH FEARLESS CONFIDENCE

We can live with fearless confidence in these times of terror, turmoil, and uncertainty as we surround our life with prayer. As we pray, we will receive a holy boldness from the Holy Spirit that enables us to speak and live the Word in these difficult days. Praying will get us through every one of the devil's attacks against us.

Pray on, Beloved!

SCRIPTURE:

"While they were praying, the place where they were meeting trembled and shook. They were all filled with the Holy Spirit and continued to speak God's Word with fearless confidence" (Acts 4:31 MSG).

PRAYER:

Father, I thank you for the privilege of prayer and the supernatural help that we receive through praying. I pray for the Holy Spirit to fill us today with a renewed confidence that displaces all fear. The devil is always scheming against us; he steals, kills, and destroys, but Jesus gives us life. We live in times when fear holds many hostage. As we spend time in prayer, give us a Word to speak along with a fearless confidence to speak it. In Jesus' name I pray, Amen.

TRUE LEADERSHIP FROM THE GREATEST LEADER

Books abound on the subject of leadership. Volumes have been written. Seminars, lectures, and course studies are everywhere, including the church.

Everyone wants to be a great leader, whether it is in the home, workplace, schoolhouse, marketplace, or church house. People look for success in current leaders and in leaders throughout history, yet there seems to be a huge vacuum of true leadership today. Where in the world are all the true leaders?

You can save yourself the time and money you might have been planning to spend on the next great leadership seminar, class, or book, because it is a simple concept: True leadership means to **serve**!

Jesus Christ is the greatest leader that has ever walked this earth. If we follow Him, we will be good leaders. What did He do? He left the riches of glory to come into our poor world to serve a lost and dying humanity. Jesus served. We are left with no greater picture of this than when Jesus took up the towel and washed dirty, stinky, nasty, un-cared-for feet. That is true leadership from The Greatest Leader.

Beloved, take up the towel and follow Jesus in serving someone today and every day. As you serve our LORD, you will become a great leader to those you are serving.

SCRIPTURE:
"Then he poured water into a basin and began to wash the disciples' feet and to wipe them with the towel that was wrapped around him" (John 13:5).

PRAYER:
Jesus, I thank you for coming into my world. You are the greatest leader that has ever walked this earth. Thank you for showing me that true leadership is all about serving humanity. Help me to not miss an opportunity to serve someone today as I serve you. The opportunities will be there; give me eyes to see them. Increase my desire to follow you by taking up the towel and serving others. In the name of Father, Son and Holy Spirit, Amen.

WHY DOES GOD NOT ANSWER MY PRAYERS?

Being in the ministry for over twenty-one years, my wife Becky and I have heard the same question over and over again. So many ask, "Why does God not answer my prayers?" They say, "I call out to Him in my time of need, but it's like He is not even there."

Please know that we must call on the Lord in truth, which means praying while expecting His promises for you as declared in His Word. It's not praying for what you want; it's praying for the promises that God has given you in His Word. So many today call on the Lord in their times of trouble, but they do not know the Word; they do not obey the Word. They ask things of the Lord that are not even in line with His Word. As we learn the Word and obey it, we can call on the Lord in truth.

When we call on the Lord in truth, we come to Him in total transparency. I'm always amazed at how some believe they can hide things from the Lord. We can hide nothing from Him. He not only has each hair on our head numbered, but He also knows our every thought, motive, action, and what is hidden in the deep recesses of our heart. Many Christians come to the Lord only in their times of trouble, trying to hide things that are not right in their lives— habitual sins, minds filled with things of the world, and hardened hearts. They call out to Him with non-repentant hearts. When He does not do what they want, they ask, "Why does God not answer my prayers?"

Those who call on the Lord in truth come to Him spiritually naked, hiding nothing. They come just as they are in total repentance, recognizing their sinfulness, being unclean in the presence of His holiness. They do not question His timing or methods in answering prayer. They simply stand on His promises. He is there to love and forgive. He is there to hear and answer. He grants them mercy while giving them grace and peace.

Beloved, call on the Lord today. He is there. He is close to all who call on Him in truth.

SCRIPTURE:
"The LORD is near to all who call on him, to all who call on him in truth" (Psalms 145:18).

PRAYER:
Father, I come to you today thanking you for always being close. You are always here with me. I come just as I am. You know my sinfulness. I'm dependent on you for your grace and mercy. Usher me into your holi-

ness today as I follow Jesus. Meet my needs according to your promises. My greatest need is more of you. Fill me with a fullness of your Holy Spirit. I long for you. In Jesus' name, Amen.

HOW TO WALK IN POWER, LOVE, AND SELF-DISCIPLINE

As we fix our eyes on Jesus and follow Him, the Holy Spirit empowers us on our journey. The Holy Spirit is our supernatural partner and is a gift from God.

In giving us the Holy Spirit, God has given us what we need to continue the point-of-need ministry of Jesus in our day. We do not walk in fear. Instead, we are given power, love, and self-discipline by the Holy Spirit.

Beloved, as you walk in the power of the Holy Spirit, you will be full of love and your life will be measured by self-discipline.

SCRIPTURE:

"God gave us a spirit not of fear but of power and love and self-control" (2 Timothy 1:7).

PRAYER:

Father, I thank you for the gift of the Holy Spirit that you give to all who follow Christ. Empower me by your Spirit today to live for Christ in a world that has gone mad. Help me reveal the love of Christ today through my words and actions. Give me the self-discipline I need to be a conqueror of every temptation that the devil throws at me. I pray in Jesus' name, Amen.

THE CURE FOR OPPRESSION AND TROUBLE

At various times throughout our lives, we all find ourselves oppressed. Trouble abounds in our day. May we constantly run to the LORD, for He is our safety!

Beloved, run into the arms of our loving LORD. He will take care of you today and forever.

SCRIPTURE:

"The Lord is a shelter for the oppressed, a refuge in times of trouble" (Psalm 9:9, NLT).

PRAYER:

Father, I thank you for the safety that is available in you. I pray today for all those who are oppressed and troubled. Comfort and strengthen them. Give us all a deep hunger for you and your Word; it is where we find guidance for all of our problems, and comfort for our souls. I pray in Jesus' name, Amen.

DAY 10

THE VALUE OF LEVEL GROUND

We experience ups and downs throughout our life. The peaks are only fleeting moments. Oh, how I long for level ground. It's on level ground where we can do our best work for the Lord. We need God to lead us to level ground on a daily basis.

I learned the value of level ground from running marathons. I have run marathons on both hilly and level terrain. Like most runners, I prefer level ground because running uphill expends a lot of energy, and running downhill is hard on the quads, especially in miles 20 through 26.2. It's hard enough for me to make it on level ground!

Some of the hills we encounter in life are unavoidable, but many are caused by us. When we go our own way and do our own thing, ignoring God as the Lord of our life, we put ourselves on a hilly course.

When we go against God's will as given to us in His Word, we create hills that are hard to endure. God doesn't do this to us. The devil doesn't do it. We do it; we choose the course of our lives. We need to learn God's will and adhere to it. God will help us if we ask. I choose to ask for His help.

Beloved, ask God to help you today and every day. He will teach you His will, and He will lead you on level ground as you obey Him.

SCRIPTURE:

"Teach me to do your will, for you are my God! Let your good Spirit lead me on level ground!" (Psalms 143:10).

PRAYER:

Father, you are my God, and I need your help. I need you to teach me to do your will. As I read your Word and apply it to my life, give me the direction I need. Forgive me for the hills I've created in my life by going my own way. I don't like hills. I desire to be led by your Holy Spirit on level ground, but I also need to be driven. Drive me by your Spirit on level ground. In Jesus' name, I pray. Amen.

DAY 11

THREE CHOICES THAT WILL START YOUR DAY OFF RIGHT EVERY DAY

Each one of us has to make lots of choices today and every day. Those choices impact our lives and the lives of those around us.

If you struggle with knowing how to keep your life on the right path, here are three choices you can make every morning that will start your day off right:

1. Choose to trust God, knowing that He loves you, and that there is nothing you can do to make Him love you any more or any less than He already does. His love for you is complete.
2. Choose to rejoice in the Lord because Jesus rescues you on a daily basis.
3. Choose to praise the Lord for His goodness toward you.

Beloved, make those three choices daily to start your day off right, and you will see your life will unfold as its meant to according to His perfect will for you.

SCRIPTURE:

"But I trust in your unfailing love. I will rejoice because you have rescued me. I will sing to the Lord because he is good to me" (Psalm 13:5-6, NLT).

PRAYER:

Father, today I choose to trust in your love for me. I choose to praise you throughout the day for your goodness toward me, knowing that you will reveal it to me many times over. I choose to rejoice in my salvation because Jesus rescues me moment by moment. Thank you for drawing me to Him. Please drive me by your Holy Spirit today to make the right choices based on your Word. I pray in Jesus' name, Amen.

HOW TO SEEK GOOD

Many people will be seeking many things today. Some will be seeking that which is good, and some will be seeking evil. Whatever is sought today will be found—whether good or evil.

When we turn on the news at the end of the day, or we pick up tomorrow's paper, we will read many accounts of those who sought evil and found it. We will see that the fruit of seeking evil is death and destruction.

Have you noticed that there is not enough news about those who seek to do good? The fruit of seeking good is life-giving; it brings hope and joy. Oh, how I wish our news would be dominated with reports of those seeking good, and not evil.

Life is the fruit of seeking good. May we daily decide to seek good instead of evil; life is there for us and others if we do.

How do we seek good? God has given us Jesus, the Good Shepherd, to follow. When Jesus walked this earth, He did good everywhere He went. He will lead us and guide us as we follow Him. As we follow Jesus, we are seeking good.

Beloved, seek good and follow Jesus. He is not far away. He is right there with you and will empower you by the Holy Spirit to do good. The fruit will be life!

SCRIPTURE:

"Seek good, and not evil, that you may live; and so the LORD, the God of hosts, will be with you, as you have said" (Amos 5:14).

PRAYER:

Father, I thank you for Jesus and the abiding presence of the Holy Spirit. As I am presented with decisions to make throughout the day, help me make the right choice in seeking good. Help me remember what Jesus would do in each situation. I choose today to seek good and not evil in everything I do. Give your life to others through me today. I pray in Jesus' name. Amen.

DAY 13

FINDING YOUR HEART

Where is your heart today? That may sound like a silly question, but it will do us good today to examine our hearts and discover what keeps them captivated.

We may find our heart in an unlikely place. We may find it in a relationship, a job, a business, a car, a house, a 401K, a bank account, or maybe in those collectables that we cherish so much. These things will eventually lead to disappointments, and ultimately, to a broken heart.

Where is your heart today?

Why is that such an important question? Because wherever our heart is found, we find our treasure.

If you find your heart in Jesus, you will never be disappointed in Him, and He will never break your heart.

Beloved, lose your heart in Jesus today, for He is a priceless treasure.

SCRIPTURE:

"Do not lay up for yourselves treasures on earth, where moth and rust destroy and where thieves break in and steal, but lay up for yourselves treasures in heaven, where neither moth nor rust destroys and where thieves do not break in and steal" (Matthew 6:19-20).

PRAYER:

Heavenly Father, forgive me for losing my heart in places where it should not be. It is easy in our day to lose sight of what is truly a treasure. I desire for my treasure to always be Jesus; He is priceless. My relationship with Jesus will never be disappointing; He will never break my heart. It is in His name that I pray. Amen.

HOW TO GUARD YOUR MOUTH

Have you ever said something that you wished you had never said? I sure have. It's not a very pleasant experience to go through.

The sixteenth president of the United States, Abraham Lincoln, was one of the greatest leaders in history. If you do much reading on him, you will find that he was a man of few words, but when he did speak, his words were usually very powerful. He once said, "Better to remain silent and be thought a fool than to speak out and remove all doubt." I've done my fair share of removing all doubt at times. How about you?

The greatest person who ever walked this earth was Jesus Christ. When Jesus spoke, the effect was powerful. His words brought life from death and turned chaos into order. I'm convinced that Jesus will help us guard our mouth if we allow Him. Guarding our mouth brings life and order.

A mentor of mine in the ministry has mastered guarding his mouth. I'm sure it has been with the help of Jesus. When he speaks, his words bring life and encouragement to the hearer.

I'm a work in progress, and still learning that guarding my mouth brings life, but Jesus is helping me. How about you? Have you mastered it? Or are you still learning? Either way, Jesus will help us as we follow Him.

Beloved, allow Jesus to help you guard your mouth today and choose your words wisely.

SCRIPTURE:

"Whoever guards his mouth preserves his life; he who opens wide his lips comes to ruin" (Proverbs 13:3).

PRAYER:

Father, I thank you for the ability to communicate through words, which is a gift you have given. Please forgive me for the times when I have misused that ability. I need your help in guarding my mouth so my words can always bring life and encouragement. Help me to know when to speak and when to be silent. When it is time to speak, give me your words and the unction to say them. Help me speak life and not death. Help me speak order and not chaos. Help hearers find encouragement in my words. In the name of Jesus, I pray. Amen.

HOW DO WE REALLY LOVE?

When my daughter was just a little girl, I played a game with her over and over again. I would say, "How much do you love me?"

She would stretch out her little arms and hands as far apart as she could while saying, "I love you this much!" Then she would ask, "How much do you love me?"

I would take my much bigger arms and hands and do the same, and say, "I love you this much!" in return.

I would utilize that opportunity to teach her a wonderful truth that Jesus has given us, while also teaching her the Biblical mandate for children to obey and honor their parents. I would tell her, "If you really love Mommy and Daddy, you will obey us. Obeying Mommy and Daddy show us that you love us."

Becky and I were not perfect parents, but we always tried to reward our children's obedience with positive reinforcement, and their disobedience with negative reinforcement. Scripture teaches that we are the children of God; likewise, there are rewards for obedience to His Word and consequences for disobedience, which is sin.

We can say that we love Jesus, but *how* do we really love Him? We love Him by doing what He says. He gives us positive reinforcement through the Holy Spirit, who will equip and empower us to live a victorious life for Him.

Beloved, reveal your love for Jesus by doing what He says. The positive reinforcement He gives by the Holy Spirit is out of this world!

SCRIPTURE:

"Jesus said, 'If you love me, you will keep my commandments. And I will ask the Father, and he will give you another Helper, to be with you forever, even the Spirit of truth, whom the world cannot receive, because it neither sees him nor knows him. You know him, for he dwells with you and will be in you'" (John 14:15-17).

PRAYER:

Heavenly Father, your love for me is perfect. As an earthly father, I have often failed at perfect love, but you have not. Sometimes, your perfect love is tough, as my sins will always separate me from your presence. That does not feel good, but you are always there when I turn to you in repentance. Thank you. Help me always to be quick and zealous in my repentance when I disobey your Word. Convict and chastise me by your Holy Spirit when I displease you. Fill me full of your Word so that I can love you more as I obey it. Thank you for all the spiritual rewards you give through the Holy Spirit as I obey. In Jesus' name, I pray. Amen.

DO YOU EVER FEEL FORGOTTEN?

We may be forgotten by some, but not by one.

1,224…

1,225…

1,226…

…You saw three hairs from your head wash down the shower drain. Oops, there goes number 1,227.

God cares so much about you that He has each hair numbered. He knows you intimately—every detail about you. He loves you. He will take care of you. There is no need to fear what may come your way. Trust Him. He has not forgotten about you.

Beloved, every time you see a hair fall out of your head or a bird flying by, be reminded that God loves you and has not forgotten you.

What do birds have to do with it?

SCRIPTURE:

"Are not five sparrows sold for two pennies? And not one of them is forgotten before God. Why, even the hairs of your head are all numbered. Fear not; you are of more value than many sparrows" (Luke 12:6-7).

PRAYER:

Father, I know today that I am not forgotten; if you care for birds, you'll care for me. Thank you for knowing me so intimately that you have even numbered the hairs on my head. I trust you and I'm confident that you will help me in all of my difficulties today, whatever may come. If I get caught up in moments of crisis today, remind me that you are with me. I pray in the precious name of Jesus. Amen

HOW TO RECEIVE ENDURANCE, ENCOURAGEMENT, AND HOPE

We live at a time when many exist in a seemingly endless state of hopelessness. The news is filled with stories of wars and rumors of wars, terrorism, anarchy, famine, drought, unemployment, economic recession, depression, disease, sickness, and an epidemic of both financial and spiritual bankruptcy. Uncertainty abounds.

During the twenty-one years I've served in the ministry, I have noticed a rapid decline in the hunger for Scripture. Many go to church, but few read, study, and memorize the Bible. Some only receive bless-me-and-make-me-feel-good sermons on Sundays that may encourage them for a brief season, but such light teaching does not build endurance. When a crisis hits, they lose hope.

Endurance, encouragement, and hope are all needed to make it in the days that we live in. We should not be shocked at how bad things have gotten, and it will get a lot worse before it gets any better. Jesus warned us of the times we are living in.

Where does one find endurance, encouragement, and hope in these difficult times? The same place we have always found it: in Scripture—God's Word—the Bible. The Bible is our source. If we do not read it, study it, and hide it in our heart, we will lose hope, and we will not endure until the end. Church attendance is not enough. We need a daily feeding of the Word of God.

Beloved, feast on God's Word and receive endurance, encouragement, and hope. It's one thing we can get fat on without becoming unhealthy.

SCRIPTURE:

"For whatever was written in former days was written for our instruction, that through endurance and through the encouragement of the Scriptures we might have hope" (Romans 15:4).

PRAYER:

Our Most Holy God, I thank you for your written Word. Not only is it your love story to us, but it also brings us the endurance, encouragement, and hope that we need every day we read it. Increase my hunger for your Word, Lord. Increase my desire to read Scripture every day, seeking everything that you have for me in it. Help me understand the Scripture I read and apply it to my life through your Holy Spirit. Help me hide your Word in my heart that I might not sin against you. I receive your endurance, encouragement, and hope today through your Word. In Jesus' name, I pray. Amen.

RECEIVING JOY IN THE MIDST OF YOUR AFFLICTION

You may find yourself in great affliction. It may be today or in the future, but when you're in the midst of affliction, you can receive the Word with the joy of the Holy Spirit.

The Apostle Paul knew affliction as he lived for Christ. He was stoned and left for dead. He was beaten multiple times. He went without food. He was shipwrecked. He was imprisoned. He was killed.

Jesus knew affliction, He was tortured; He suffered; He bled; and He died on an old rugged cross.

Paul and Jesus had something in common other than affliction—joy. They both had the joy of the Holy Spirit.

Beloved, in the midst of our afflictions, we have the joy of the Holy Spirit. It defies logic. It's a gift from God.

SCRIPTURE:

"And you became imitators of us and of the Lord, for you received the word in much affliction, with the joy of the Holy Spirit" (1 Thessalonians 1:6).

PRAYER:

Heavenly Father, I thank you for the joy that comes by your Holy Spirit. It carries me through times of great affliction. Give me that joy today as I receive your Word into my heart. When affliction comes, may others see this joy and desire its source. I pray in the name of Jesus. Amen.

WHEN PERSECUTION COMES

Some people will not like the fact that you follow Christ and continue His point-of-need ministry through the power of the Holy Spirit. Along the way you will be rejected by some. It may happen at work, school, or at home. Persecution may come from a relative, a boss, a schoolmate, a coworker, a friend, or a complete stranger.

When persecution comes, don't worry about what you will say. Jesus will help you through the Holy Spirit. He promised this to His early followers, knowing they would witness and live through the destruction of Jerusalem. This same promise is for His followers today.

Beloved, be strong and stand firm in your faith. Your endurance in Christ will save you.

SCRIPTURE:

"But before all this they will lay their hands on you and persecute you, delivering you up to the synagogues and prisons, and you will be brought before kings and governors for my name's sake. This will be your opportunity to bear witness. Settle it therefore in your minds not to meditate beforehand how to answer, for I will give you a mouth and wisdom, which none of your adversaries will be able to withstand or contradict. You will be delivered up even by parents and brothers and relatives and friends, and some of you they will put to death. You will be hated by all for my name's sake. But not a hair of your head will perish. By your endurance you will gain your lives" (Luke 21:12-19).

PRAYER:

Precious Father, give me the strength I need today to stand firm in my faith no matter what someone says or does to me. I'm confident that Jesus will help me as I follow Him. I thank you in advance for the words to say, and for your protection and endurance. It's all through Jesus and by the Holy Spirit that I am able to live for you. In Jesus' name, I pray. Amen.

HOW TO ENDURE TIMES OF SUFFERING

How do we love God? We obey Him. We delight greatly in His commands.

Loving God will lead us to a cross we must bear. The cross is indicative of suffering.

Jesus obeyed the Father and suffered a painful death an old rugged cross. Loving the Father, He simply went about doing good, yet He suffered. His suffering is not fully comprehensible to us. He was tortured to a point that no ordinary person could withstand. Stripped naked, beaten, and spat upon, He hung nailed to a cross, suffering until death—crucified, yet innocent of any wrongdoing.

How can any good come from suffering? It's hard to see when we are in the midst of suffering. It goes against the prevalent "bless-me" theology that is proclaimed from many pulpits across the land. Suffering is hardly ever touched on in some churches. The simple truth of the Bible is that we will suffer as we love God. We will suffer as we deny ourselves, take up our cross, and follow Jesus in total obedience. There will be seasons of tremendous blessings, but suffering cannot be avoided on our journey from earth to heaven's glory.

How do we endure times of suffering? We will endure as we keep our eyes fixed on Jesus. Good came from His suffering, although His followers at the time could not see any good in His violent crucifixion. Soon they would discover that His suffering and death led to His resurrection and ascension into heaven. Death had been defeated, once and for all, and we have the opportunity to receive life—abundant and eternal.

Beloved, good will come from suffering. In fact, as you love God, He is working all things together for good. You can trust that promise, as you love Him.

SCRIPTURE:

"And we know that for those who love God all things work together for good, for those who are called according to his purpose" (Romans 8:28).

PRAYER:

Father, I thank you for the promises in your Word that I can hold on to as I love you and follow Jesus. Knowing that suffering is part of the life of a Christ follower, your promise to work all things together for good gives me much peace. Thank you for fulfilling that promise in my life, as I love you. I pray in Jesus' precious name. Amen.

HOW TO GET YOUR REST

REST — a four letter word that signifies some-thing most of us do not get enough of.

Many people work hard to earn a living. Many are under tremendous amounts of stress—at work, at school, and in the home. There are so many single parents today raising children without the additional help of a spouse. Many grandparents are raising grandchildren. Some take care of an aging parent or spouse as well. It's important to take time out to rest.

God did not design our minds and our bodies to go non-stop. Working hard is honorable, but without rest, we will have a mental or physical breakdown. Our bodies were designed by God to require rest in order to stay healthy.

Take one day a week and rest. God did. After He created, He rested. Did God need the rest because He got tired and grew weary? No, God does not get tired. God doesn't even take power naps, but God rested a day, giving us an example to follow, knowing the limitations of our created bodies.

Beloved, do not neglect your rest. Take one day a week and rest, regenerate, refuel, and recuperate, reflecting on the work that you have accomplished. Be thankful to God and rest, Beloved.

SCRIPTURE:

"Thus the heavens and the earth were finished, and all the host of them. And on the seventh day God finished his work that he had done, and he rested on the seventh day from all his work that he had done. So God blessed the seventh day and made it holy, because on it God rested from all his work that he had done in creation." (Genesis 2:1-3).

PRAYER:

Father, please forgive me for all the times I have not taken a Sabbath rest. Help me to look past what needs to be done, taking one day a week to rest and refuel. I don't want to burn out, nor do I want my work and my ministry to fizzle out; there is too much to be accomplished for your Kingdom. In Jesus' name, I pray. Amen.

BEING DELIVERED, TRANSFERRED, REDEEMED, AND FORGIVEN

The Christ follower is delivered, transferred, redeemed, and forgiven. Wow! That is something to get excited about! Read that first sentence again and allow the Holy Spirit to speak to your heart today.

God loves us so much that He sent Jesus to deliver us from the darkness and bondage of sin. At the cross, Jesus broke the power of sin. Because He did, sin has no dominion over those who follow Jesus. Jesus is our deliverer!

The moment we place our faith in Jesus, we are transferred from the kingdom of darkness to the Kingdom of light—God's Kingdom where Christ rules and reigns at the right hand of His Father. Our time of being captive to sin is over, and we have a new place to dwell.

Delivering us from sin and transferring us into His Kingdom came with a price—the shedding of Jesus' life-giving blood. By shedding His own precious blood, Jesus redeemed us, which means He bought us out of the slavery of sin. We are blood bought. The blood of Jesus is more precious and more valuable than all the gold in this world. Gold cannot redeem us, but the blood of Christ can.

Forgiveness comes as we confess our sins and run into the loving arms of Jesus. All of our sins are forgiven and forgotten. We get a fresh start and a supernatural partner who will help us overcome all of our sins.

Beloved, you have been delivered from darkness, transferred to His Kingdom, redeemed by His blood, and forgiven of your sins. It's all through Jesus, and it's made available to you because God loves you. Be delivered, transferred, redeemed, and forgiven!

SCRIPTURE:

"He has delivered us from the domain of darkness and transferred us to the kingdom of his beloved Son, in whom we have redemption, the forgiveness of sins" (Colossians 1:13-14).

PRAYER:

My loving heavenly Father, I thank you for delivering me from the bondage of sin. I thank you for transferring me from the darkness of sin into the light of your Kingdom. I thank you for redeeming me with the precious blood of your Son. I thank you for forgiving me for sinning against you and others. Help me serve you today with gratitude and dedication because you have delivered me, transferred me, redeemed me, and forgiven me. I pray in your Son's name. Amen.

DAY 23

A SUPERNATURAL GUIDE

After His resurrection, Jesus left earth to return to the Father, but He promised not to leave His followers without help. Christ followers are helped on their own journey from earth to glory by the Holy Spirit—the Helper Jesus has sent to us.

The Father, Son, and Holy Spirit work as one. May we comprehend this and rely on the Holy Spirit as the Helper we have been given to ensure that we have a successful journey through life no matter how bumpy the ride might be along the way.

The Holy Spirit brings love, power, and self-discipline into the lives of those who follow Christ. The Holy Spirit helps us understand as we read and hear the Word of God, and when we allow Him to do so, the Holy Spirit will guide us into all the truth of Jesus, both now and in the future. We will know it is truth when it lines up with the Word. This is what Jesus told His first followers before He went to the cross, and it was fulfilled in their lives afterward. It is still being fulfilled in each Christ follower today.

Beloved, as you read the Bible and pray today, ask the Holy Spirit to guide you into all the truth of Jesus, both now and in the future. We have within us a deposit of the glory that is to come. May we comprehend and rely on the Holy Spirit, the Helper we have been given for safely navigating our earthly journey as we make our way homeward to heaven.

SCRIPTURE:

"When the Spirit of truth comes, he will guide you into all the truth, for he will not speak on his own authority, but whatever he hears he will speak, and he will declare to you the things that are to come" (John 16:13).

PRAYER:

Jesus, I thank you for not forsaking me. Thank you for sending the Holy Spirit to indwell me and to help me on my journey from earth to glory. I pray that you will lead me into all of your truth, both now and in the future, by the Holy Spirit. Give me ears to hear what He will speak to me today. Amen.

THREE TIMES WHEN YOU ARE LIKELY TO BE TEMPTED

Satan is always looking for ways to tempt you and trip you up, but there are three times when you can count on him coming at you full force:

1. When you set your focus on seeking more of God
2. When you are physically weak
3. When you think you know the Word

When you are seeking more of God, Satan will try to distract you. When you go without rest and are physically weak, you are very vulnerable to temptation. When you think you know the Word, Satan will twist the Word to deceive you and lead you astray.

Beloved, the devil seeks to destroy you. If he tempted Jesus, you can count on him tempting you as you follow Jesus. As we learn his tactics, we can better defend against them, and be better equipped for victory. Keep your eyes fixed on Jesus!

SCRIPTURE:

"Then Jesus was led up by the Spirit into the wilderness to be tempted by the devil. And after fasting forty days and forty nights, he was hungry. And the tempter came and said to him, 'If you are the Son of God, command these stones to become loaves of bread.' But he answered, 'It is written, "Man shall not live by bread alone, but by every word that comes from the mouth of God."' Then the devil took him to the holy city and set him on the pinnacle of the temple and said to him, 'If you are the Son of God, throw yourself down, for it is written, "He will command his angels concerning you," and "On their hands they will bear you up, lest you strike your foot against a stone."' Jesus said to him, 'Again it is written, "You shall not put the Lord your God to the test."' Again, the devil took him to a very high mountain and showed him all the kingdoms of the world and their glory. And he said to him, 'All these I will give you, if you will fall down and worship me.' Then Jesus said to him, 'Be gone, Satan! For it is written, "You shall worship the Lord your God and him only shall you serve."' Then the devil left him, and behold, angels came and were ministering to him" (Matthew 4:1-11).

PRAYER:

Father, I ask you to deliver me from temptation today. Help me to grow stronger in your Word. I thank you for the example you gave us of Christ overcoming temptation. Continue to enlighten me to the tactics of the devil so that I can be on guard and ready to defend against them. Strengthen me by your Holy Spirit. I pray in Jesus' name. Amen.

THREE WAYS TO WIN OVER TEMPTATION

Here is some exciting news: We can live victoriously! There are three ways to win over temptation:
1. Rely on the Holy Spirit.
2. Know God's Word.
3. Apply God's Word.

First of all, please realize that temptation is not sin. Temptation does not become sin unless you give in to the temptation. As long as you have a heartbeat, breath within your nostrils, and are conscious, you will be tempted. There is no greater example of overcoming temptation than when Jesus was tempted by Satan.

Jesus was taken into the wilderness by the Holy Spirit, where He was tested. To win over temptation, Jesus relied on the Holy Spirit, His knowledge of God's Word, and His ability to apply God's Word to everything Satan brought against Him. Beloved, the same will work for us as we follow Christ.

SCRIPTURE:

"Then Jesus was led up by the Spirit into the wilderness to be tempted by the devil. And after fasting

53

forty days and forty nights, he was hungry. And the tempter came and said to him, 'If you are the Son of God, command these stones to become loaves of bread.' But he answered, 'It is written, "Man shall not live by bread alone, but by every word that comes from the mouth of God."' Then the devil took him to the holy city and set him on the pinnacle of the temple and said to him, 'If you are the Son of God, throw yourself down, for it is written, "He will command his angels concerning you," and "On their hands they will bear you up, lest you strike your foot against a stone."' Jesus said to him, 'Again it is written, "You shall not put the Lord your God to the test."' Again, the devil took him to a very high mountain and showed him all the kingdoms of the world and their glory. And he said to him, 'All these I will give you, if you will fall down and worship me.' Then Jesus said to him, 'Be gone, Satan! For it is written, "You shall worship the Lord your God and him only shall you serve."' Then the devil left him, and behold, angels came and were ministering to him" (Matthew 4:1-11).

PRAYER:
Father, I thank you for the victorious example Jesus gave us when He overcame Satan's temptation in the wilderness. Help me rely on the Holy Spirit and your Word as temptation comes my way today. Help me to live victoriously, being an example to those around me as I follow Christ. I pray this in His name. Amen.

WHERE TO FIND SAFETY IN A WORLD GONE MAD

Corruption, greed, sexual immorality, violence — we live in a world that has grown increasingly out of step with God and His Word. Many today believe in God but do not live in obedience to His Word. In such a culture, is it possible to live fully for God? Yes, it is, as shown in the life of Noah. Jesus compared our day to the days of Noah.

In the midst of all the sin of Noah's day, he lived righteously, and his everlasting testimony is that he found favor with God. When God brought His wrath upon the inhabitants of the earth as penalty for their sinful ways, He spared Noah and his family and provided salvation for them through Noah's obedience to God's Word to build an ark of safety.

Beloved, as you follow Christ in total obedience and abandonment, you live righteously, finding favor with God through Jesus Christ. God's family, in which you are a member through Jesus, will be spared the wrath of God to come upon this earth. Let Jesus be your ark, the One you go to for safety. You will have an everlasting testimony of finding favor with God, walking with Him, and living righteously in the midst of a world that has gone mad.

Continue to run to Jesus; He is your salvation.

SCRIPTURE:

"The LORD saw that the wickedness of man was great in the earth, and that every intention of the thoughts of his heart was only evil continually. And the LORD was sorry that he had made man on the earth, and it grieved him to his heart. So the LORD said, 'I will blot out man whom I have created from the face of the land, man and animals and creeping things and birds of the heavens, for I am sorry that I have made them.' But Noah found favor in the eyes of the LORD. These are the generations of Noah. Noah was a righteous man, blameless in his generation. Noah walked with God" (Genesis 6:5-9).

PRAYER:

My just and righteous heavenly Father, I thank you today for giving me salvation in Jesus Christ, instead of what I deserve. Jesus is my ark, and I run to Him for safety. I give myself to Him today for His service. Use me as you will, and give me your instructions to follow in the midst of a world that has gone mad. In Jesus' name, I pray. Amen.

HOW YOU CAN PUT SIN TO DEATH

Followers of Jesus Christ are brothers and sisters. We have been birthed into the family of God by the Holy Spirit. As Christ followers and family members, we have an obligation to live by the Spirit and not the flesh.

It is by the Holy Spirit that we can put sin to death. The Holy Spirit gives us the necessary self-discipline to live victoriously. As we rely on the Holy Spirit, we will be empowered to overcome sinful lifestyles that the flesh desires. Reliance upon the Holy Spirit will break the habitual sin that seeks to bind and destroy all those who live by the flesh.

Take a moment to ponder this truth: If the Holy Spirit is powerful enough to give us a new birth in a new family, He is powerful enough to help us overcome the desires of the flesh.

Beloved, rely on the Holy Spirit today. Rely on the Holy Spirit. He will strengthen you.

SCRIPTURE:

"Therefore, brothers and sisters, we have an obligation—but it is not to the sinful nature, to live according to it. For if you live according to the sinful nature, you will die; but if by the Spirit you put to death the misdeeds of the body, you will live" (Romans 8:12-13 TNIV).

PRAYER:
Holy Spirit, I need you today and every day. I cannot overcome the flesh without your supernatural help. Fill me today with your power. Bring to memory Scripture I've read and studied, and help me apply it to every situation I will face today. Increase my hunger for the Word, which is my sword. Increase my desire for holy living in these unholy times. Live through me today. In the name of the Father, Son, and Holy Spirit, Amen.

HOW TO FEAR THE LORD

When the Bible says that we are to "fear the LORD," it means to delight greatly in His commandments. The Word says, "Praise the LORD! Blessed is the man who fears the LORD, who greatly delights in his commandments!" (Psalms 112:1).

According to Psalms 112:1, whenever you see the phrase, "fear the LORD" in the Bible, you can substitute it with the phrase, "delight in His commandments." The Bible also tells us that delighting in His commandments is the beginning of wisdom: "The fear of the LORD is the beginning of wisdom, and the knowledge of the Holy One is insight" (Proverbs 9:10).

The person who fears the LORD will have a hunger for God's Word and will search it as though searching for hidden treasure to discover the wisdom and instruction found in its pages. According to Jesus, we reveal our love for Him by obeying the commandments in His Word. Jesus said, "If you love me, you will keep my commandments" (John 14:15).

The main problem in today's society is not lack of the Word (God's commandments). The problem is that there is a famine of *hearing* the Word. Amos prophesied, "Behold, the days are coming," declares the Lord GOD, "when I will send a famine on the land—not a famine of bread, nor a thirst for water, but of hearing the words of the LORD" (Amos 8:11).

We are living in those days that Amos prophesied about. Today, with churches on almost every street corner in America and Bibles in almost every home, there is not as much of a famine of the Word as there is a famine of hearing the words of the LORD. Many do not fear the Lord; they are not delighting in His commandments. They determine right from wrong based on what feels right instead of fearing the LORD (delighting in His commandments). God's word refers to those as fools: "The fear of the LORD is the beginning of knowledge; fools despise wisdom and instruction" (Proverbs 1:7).

I dream of a day when people will not just delight in His blessings, but will also delight in His commandments—fearing the LORD.

Beloved, continue to fear the LORD — delight in His commandments.

PRAYER:

Father, I thank you for giving us your Word. Give us ears to hear in our day what the Spirit is speaking through your Word. I choose today to be a student of your Word, greatly delighting in your commandments. I pray for a great revival to shake the land. May it begin within churches. Give us a hunger for your Word, resulting in us delighting in the commandments much more than desiring the blessings. In Jesus' name I pray, Amen.

DAY 29

THE SOLUTION TO WORRY

Don't worry. How many times have you been told that? It's one of those things that is easier said than done, isn't it?

God teaches us throughout the Bible not to worry. Instead, He wants us to learn to trust Him completely with everything. If He said, "Don't worry," but left us without a solution, it would be very hard to get through the difficulties of life. However, because He loves and cares for us, He gives us the solution to worry—prayer and thanksgiving.

It is through prayer that we release all of our burdens to God. We do this daily and in our times of need. We take all of our worries, needs, and requests to Him in prayer. As we do, we receive His grace and mercy.

It is through thanksgiving that we identify all the difficulties He has brought us through in the past. We remember all the prayers He has answered and the strength that He has given when we didn't think we could go another step on our journey. We remember how He has provided for us in the past through employment, shelter, food, clothing, and encouragement at times when we've so desperately needed it.

We thank Him for ALL that He has done, and we trust that He will do it again.

Beloved, don't worry. In a world gone mad, God is in control. Take full advantage of the privilege of prayer. Give thanksgiving to God for all that He has done. He will do it again.

SCRIPTURE:

"Do not be anxious about anything, but in everything by prayer and supplication with thanksgiving let your requests be made known to God" (Philippians 4:6).

PRAYER:

Father, I come to you today in prayer with thanksgiving. You have been so good to me, providing all my needs. I thank you for the answers to prayer that I've seen. I thank you for the grace and mercy you give me in my time of need. I thank you for the privilege of prayer. I thank you for taking my burdens and meeting my needs today. In Jesus' name, I pray. Amen.

DAY 30

REMEMBER WHO YOUR WORDS AND ACTIONS REPRESENT

In our days of lawsuits and litigation, we read and hear many disclaimers. One common disclaimer goes something like this: *These views and opinions may not necessarily represent the views and opinions of fill-in-the-blank*. The fill-in-the-blank may be a television station or network, a company, a magazine, a newspaper, or even a church blog or newsletter.

As Christ followers, we represent Jesus Christ, and there is no disclaimer about that. We confess Him as our Lord and our Savior. We are not perfect, and we make mistakes along the way, but He is not concerned about lawsuits and litigation. He gives no disclaimer as we represent Him. When we say or do something that He does not approve of, He will correct us. He disciplines us because He loves us. He is constantly molding us into His likeness as we follow Him. We are a work in progress, but each step we take with Him, gets us closer to the finished product. The best is yet to come!

Beloved, represent Jesus today in all that you say and do. He will help you, and you will be able to give

God the Father thanks through Him. Jesus can do within you and through you what none other can do.

SCRIPTURE:

"And whatever you do, in word or deed, do everything in the name of the Lord Jesus, giving thanks to God the Father through him" (Colossians 3:17).

PRAYER:

Father, as I go about my day today, remind me that I'm to represent Jesus in all that I say and do. Help me to guard my words and my actions. I give you thanks today through Jesus, and it is in His name that I pray. Amen.

ABOUT THE AUTHOR – GREGORY A. JOHNSON

Gregory A. Johnson answered God's call into public ministry in 1988. He is a Christ follower with a strong desire to reach, encourage, and equip people to continue the point-of-need ministry of Jesus, extending it outside the walls of a church building and beyond the confines of a church service. In addition to fulfilling the demanding duties of being a pastor, husband, and father, Greg has ministered in the streets, to the homeless, to those in jail, in transitional homes for those coming out of prison, and in correctional facilities for gang members.

In both his writing and public speaking, Greg brings messages from the throne of God as true spiritual meat for every hungry reader and listener. The messages are relevant, life changing, convicting, and blessed by God's precious grace.

Greg is an ordained minister with over three decades of service in the nonprofit, private, and public sectors. In addition to being a church pastor since 1991, he has worked for two Fortune 400 companies as well as with the Governor's Office for Technology in the Commonwealth of Kentucky. His education includes a Bachelor of Science degree in Computer Science from

Gregory A. Johnson

Marshall University, Huntington, West Virginia; post-graduate work in Business Administration at Xavier University, Cincinnati, Ohio; Diploma in Ministerial Studies from Global University, Springfield, Missouri; and Certificate in Management Fundamentals from the Government Services Center at Kentucky State University, Frankfort, Kentucky. In 2003, Johnson was conferred a Kentucky Colonel by Governor Paul E. Patton, Commonwealth of Kentucky.

Greg's first book, _The Characters of Christmas: God at Work in Our Lives_, was published in December 2010. He is currently working on additional book projects.

Greg and His wife Becky have been married since March 1982, and God has blessed them with two children, Austin and Kelsey. The Johnsons reside in the Commonwealth of Kentucky. You can connect with Greg at http://www.GregoryAJohnson.com.

BIBLE TRANSLATIONS

46432364R00046

Made in the USA
Lexington, KY
03 November 2015